# Breakfast at Mel's

Also by Douglas Lochhead

The Heart Is Fire (1959)
An Old Woman Looks Out on Gabarus Bay
Remembering History (1959)
It Is All Around (1960)
Shepherds before Kings (1963)
Poet Talking (1964)
A & B & C &: An Alphabet (1969)
Millwood Road Poems (1970)
Prayers in a Field (1974)
The Full Furnace: Collected Poems (1975)
High Marsh Road: Lines for a Diary (1980, 1996)
A & E: A Long Poem (1980)
Battle Sequence (1980)
The Panic Field (1984)
Tiger in the Skull: New and Selected Poems (1986)
Upper Cape Poems (1989)
Dykelands (1989)
Black Festival (1991)
Homage to Henry Alline (1992)
Charlie, Boo Boo, Nutley and Clutch: Twelve Canadian
Jollies, Lovelies (1997)

# Breakfast at Mel's

## and other poems
## of love and places

### DOUGLAS LOCHHEAD

GOOSE LANE

Published by Goose Lane Editions with the assistance of the Canada
Council, the Department of Canadian Heritage, and the New
Brunswick Department of Municipalities, Culture and Housing,
1997.

Some of these poems have appeared in: *The Antigonish Review,
Canadian Literature, The Cormorant, The New Brunswick Reader* and
*The Angelica Series* of The Purple Wednesday Society. To the editors
of these journals I extend my warm appreciation.

Photos of Mel's Tea Room (established 1919), Bridge Street,
Sackville, New Brunswick, Canada, by Syamal Mitra.
Back cover photo by Kenneth Lochhead.
Cover and book design by Julie Scriver.
Printed in Canada by Tribune Printing.
10  9  8  7  6  5  4  3  2

Canadian Cataloguing in Publication Data

Lochhead, Douglas, 1922 -
    Breakfast at Mel's and other poems of love and places
    ISBN 0-86492-228-0

I. Title.

PS8523.O33B73 1997        C811'.54        C97-950042-7
PR9199.3.L63B73 1997

Goose Lane Editions
469 King Street
Fredericton New Brunswick
CANADA   E3B 1E5

To Mel's

&

for Phyllis

with special appreciation to
Roger and Marilyn Goodwin
&
Bernard and Minerva Goodwin
of Mel's

Everything flows and nothing abides;
everything gives way and nothing is fixed.
HERACLITUS


The invariable mark of wisdom
is to see the miraculous in the common.
EMERSON

# Contents

*The Bite of Love*

## Love Sequence of Sorts

## Randoms

# Breakfast at Mel's

# Breakfast at Mel's

We are here to celebrate,
    to celebrate just about everything.

*Are we ready to order?*

    Is it time? Yes, it is time
    if we would speak that way . . .

*What will you have?*

    I'll have your mouth,
        your arms . . .
    You may have the same.


SMALL DRINKS AND ICE CREAM
CONES WILL BE SERVED AT THE
FOUNTAIN ONLY.

        It is only right.


Yes, here we are where old loves,
    speaking of time, send echoes
    over the booths, over the fountain,
    to rest among the pumpkins
    and the freshest eggs in town
    in those wide windows . . .

In a few days you will be here,
this is a practice run.

*I'll have two fried eggs with bacon.*


BROKEN OR MISSING DISHES WILL BE
CHARGED TO THE CUSTOMER.


Now I hold your hand
    just as I will when you arrive.
    It is always the time business.
    How appropriate for a tea room.
    How many hands have held
    right where we are sitting?
    You will love it here,
    it is an institution,
    it is a Sandwich Bar
    where you and I will plan
    our days and nights.

*Yes, I will have coffee. No,*
*make it tea. This is a Tea Room.*

Perhaps we should dance
    when we are finally together.
    Should I take
              the preliminary steps?


CUSTOMERS WILL BE HELD RESPONSIBLE
FOR ANY DAMAGE TO FURNISHINGS,
BROKEN OR MISSING DISHES, ETC.


There are warnings everywhere
    which I will take notice of
    until you come, then life
    may change, may lead us
    into a devil's tango, a romp
    around the Video Lotto machine,
    up against Mr. Ganong's candy stand,
    it is all too wonderful
              to contemplate.

Yes, it is a question of time,
    of those old echoes up and down
              the aisles.

The wonderful ladies from the Bank
across the street make up the present,
but they are leaving now
and you, my love, will come in time
for breakfast.

*Roger of Mel's*

# Love in Places

# Love in Places

## 1

A dark summons, or did you think of it
that way? For me there were no banners
but only the arrows of your words
with their bright flames breaking
the night like scarring stars.
At Stromness we went ashore.
Venus stood in the doorway.
There were ghost ships.

## 2

Your shoulders, arms, our tropic talk
as lovers, such warm evidence lingers.
Testimony of the past. You said
I expect too much, too soon. More questions.
Do you remember, as you must,
a leopard skin upon the floor?
The thin, morning noise of sugar birds?
Flamingo flowers?

## 3

Slow time under a slow sun.
Is this the never-never land?
I mean the passing place where you,
appearing now so seldom, if at all,
put down your wings? Let it be.
Westward it is in a lean of men and horses.
Rounds of drinks under pavilions.
A mocking time of travel.

**4**

Bugaboo lips. Tongue as helicopter.
Avalanches of passion. Walk out in the spring.
Upon the table proof piles as snow.
Leave it I hear you say under questioning.
Now let us find for ourselves more ways
without counting. Bed jokes.
Bougainvillea blossoms turn in the air
just here where I am sitting.

## 5

Love on the marsh Yorkshire style.
Hot buns in a Ram truck.
Against Etter Ridge the wind holds itself
while the tongue of Fundy speaks
of the tight balance of our days. Is it time?
Now the chair is empty.
The guard changes on the fortress hill.
Silent parade.

## 6

Words slip away like loose shale
leaving me grizzled. So be it, you say.
At least you can take a stand.
The same time over and over. Turning
the pages of my tired performance.
Let us meet at The Vienna.
Let us talk above distortions of old warriors.
What does love mean on Christmas cards?

## 7

The senses bend and toil
over life's long translation:
given your limp hand held to the light
with the anguish of your breasts,
part of our animal heave and ho;
while outside there are first robins
with scraping pheasants by the hemlocks.
Melting ice drives us into waiting corners.

## 8

Ambush of night thoughts in a field
of torrid frenzy. A cottage on Harris
with cold sea-rain against windows
is what I remember. You stood with me
keeping a shared watch, a warm longing
that it would not end. White love
in a loft it was. Simple.
On its other side the island is swept with sand.

## 9

What else in the telling zone of love
leaks through the holes of memory?
Love at first night. It was all a joke.
No laughter-limits. A knee-whack
of passion in a Toronto parking lot.
A commissionaire pushed a flashlight.
Nothing really going on was said.
You laughed at the truth of it.

## 10

Through a spill of spring branches
a dark face of cloud moves.
Sackville is a place of flattened foundries
where the town wharf has filled in and
gone sick with shadows of old ships.
Here cold loves bang and wave as tokens.
There is talk of closures.
Take my hand.

# Wood Point Poems

# Wood Point Poems

## 1

The leaves are dying.
The leaves are dead.
A sudden spill
of birch-gold,
of maple-blood
across the ground.
There is fog caught up
at Peck's Point.
An evening gathers
the houses in.
It is the time.
What time?
The echoed question.
Etching on hard ground.
Stiff trees
plundered by winds.
By the sayings of season.

It is colder.
Advice is to bring in
the dried roots
of summer.
They will keep.
Even the leaves
in their final places.

The great bay
will go on
in its own way.
Fog will be gone
from the point
tomorrow.

## 2

Did you see?
Did you see
the blue heron?
Or something like it?
One is usually
right there
almost to the end
of the month.
November will
see it gone.

It has been
a difficult year.
Just as others.
Everything is going.
Ice is a promise
for any morning.

Imagine the waves
frozen in breaking.
They leap
and are caught.
They form,
are thrown up
as severed sculptures.
Leftovers from
a frightened sea.
It cannot be.

Yet it is all
so very natural
after a time.
Ice-floes subdued.
Natural breaks
in the bay's calm.

The taking gulls
measure the narrow beach.
Catches of wild
bobbing chatter.
They keep
to themselves.

## 3

The dry dykes.
Two lines of them,
their skeletal
whale statement
of past packing,
piling up.
They stand
where the bay
has backed off.

A local marking.
Another.
A hunch of rain
over Chignecto.
Lone grey rider,
a leaving
over the present sea.

# 4

Snow fields
leading
to brown sea

a coiling landscape
turning itself
inward.

Burrows.
The last hay
in bales.

Some kind
of toiling
endeavour.

Too much for barns.

Left.

Give out
ye winter gods.
Your almanac
of frozen days
unclips the spirit.

White knees
in a wait
and praying place.
Then comes
an orange warmth.

Basement light
at the Wood Point
Baptist Church.
Garden
of hope
in a surround
of winter.

## 5

Tide out.
Forty feet.
Yes.

Estabrooks'
lobster boat
is on its side
in the brown
tide-gulch.

The floating umbilical
wharf lies quiet
waiting
for the coming in.

By halves
a muddy slope
for Captain E
and the rest
of us.
Clouds join
over his yellow
house.

Two plastic
butterflies.
Silent pair.
Up for Christmas.
For all days
until winds,
the almost final winds,
nip them loose.

On the other side
the tidal stream
is brown and empty.

But there is promise.

Promise of the turning
running tide.
Of something
it may or may not
bring.

## 6

I came here
to tell.
Another way
to cry.

Something to tell
you.
But the Wood Point
wind and a collage
of crazy clouds
did something.
I fell apart
into a shout
heard by no one.

Believe me
it was not
worth hearing.
But I will tell
you about it.
All about
what happened
should it somehow,
you know,
come back.

Who is to tell
the sea, that yawning,
smirking, two-tone
place?

And clouds?
Their stricken silences
up there
do me in.

Here I am again
this day.
This very place.
What numbs me
now is like
a tossed sleep.

There you are:
cliffs, waters,
waves bringing up.
No, go home,
come back
tomorrow,
early.

The young smell
the old.
And tell about it.
The old
know better.

## 7

By night.
Was it some time
on Halloween?
What is happening?

I am limp.
Loose
as porch props.
Old supposed coots
dressed up
in/as wherewithalls.
Rockers for codgers.
Pumpkin window-palaces.

What is going on
out there?

The dress-up night
is laced with rain.

Cold from basin.

Fathering fathers
drive
to Wheatons, Towers,
Hicks and Woods,
Estabrooks, Snowdons.
What fleeting generations
out of Yorkshire.
Here, now,
on the Wood Point slopes.

All a blur.

Night comes and goes.
Goes from open doorways.
Broken faces.
Groups of little greedies.
Now another.

Sparks die
in candled pumpkins.

All this was earlier
in a half-remembered year.

## 8

Sunrise.
Drop last night
in the weather.
Glitters of small ice
in hollows.

November coming
and going.

Stage set of cattle
around
the barn door.
Montage.
Old sculptures
in cold
and hot blood.

Brown solitudes.

Stowed in their places.
Together and apart.

We knock about
in the herd.
Uncorked
distant bellows
come
as steamy whispers.
Impossibles.

But what is real
about it all
is our waiting
at some great door
to let winter in.

## 9

Wild clowns.
Chariots of cloud.
How they touch
or miss
our lives.

One outdoes
the rest.

Over the top
as a last word
throws shadows
on fields of sea.

No ice at Peck's Point.
No ice from rumbling currents
of tides.
No words dropped
from mouths
of winter gods.

Wood Point lies
white and taken.

More questions of ice,
of late rallying snows
rising from done fields
about Cumberland.

## 10

The old of the year.
But there is the young
of it.
The Birth.

The web and light
straining through
and over it
to make a star.

Such huddling
in places.

Someone talked
of an inn.
Quiet bells
of camels.
A wreath of rumour
about it all.

Lights over the point.
A birth. Midnight cries.
Green mask, robes
and shoes.
The choir gathers
from the Baptist Church.

Voices fly warm
and away
over the armoured sea.

*The Bite of Love*

# The Bite of Love

## 1

Rumble over the land.
Thunder brings a heavy talk.
You still listen. It is a surprise
given the time we take.

Your hand against the heart.
Posture I can't forget.
Unconscious. Not a pose.
The hand holds a flame of grief.
My eyes are blown candles.

Empty windows in fading light
create a black stare.
Over the world, beyond the fence out there.

## 2

A bare-faced love. All of it.
Now we go groping to survive.
There are broken moments.
Ragged waiting times. Edges.

Do you remember? You ask.
Well I try. Facing the wall
waiting for a sky to turn
into old flights. Turned memories.

The night is a long bruise.
We bend into each other. Plans.
But I know you. You know me.
Something will happen. Laughter.

## 3

In the marsh there are ruins.
Houses. French drydock.
Bones of foxes, men and cattle.
Mushrooms pursue them.

Now you come out of a farm road
Dust aches in your quiet-place eyes.
I gather a round of blue flags
from a far field. Tributes.

We find in our hands a celebration.
At least my translation staggers
that way in your gone shadow.

## 4

To turn a back. Never.
There will be long silences,
slow surfacing, a kind of timing
which leaves you and me
waiting in chosen places.

The harrier's wing heals.
There are foxes in that barn.
What is happening out there?
What goings on. Old questions.

There will be signs. Signals
will flash from the bridge.
We will sail out. Somehow.

# 5

Rubberneck loves. Stretching
across far frontiers into close woods.
The summer marsh grass is cut.
It will grow again by August.

You are mother earth. Love flies
from your apron. Birds streak banners
across wet lands.

Now let's try again.
There are warm pools to touch,
to brush with our hands. Now.

## 6

A quilt waves in the wind.
"Reason over Passion" it says
telling the mind (imagine) to take over,
truss up the steaming hands.

It isn't so bad, come to think of it,
as here we are arm-locked
and heaving. A bedroom
of wild rose, fireweed, a set place
of beauty it is, you know.

Come, whisper to me, I need your lips
and a quiet spill of words.
What did you say?

7

Old bones, the tired saws and verities
rumble as clouds full of change
where great lights and darks dance
in a garden waiting for colours.

Love under a dome. Love is patchwork.
Those grinning folds of mouth and breasts
take me in. What did you say?
My time is now for listening.

Will there be a clanging over the fields
or a whimper I reach for but cannot hear?

## 8

I remember that certain angle
of your face, as close as that,
a special sun, in darkness
we contrived, preferred.

Yes, your eyes gave me
the first turning message
of that inner place, soul's
focus, embracing colour.

# 9

Pushing, knocking numbers of clouds
over the flats as galaxies of sail,
kingdoms of white mystery continuing,
making the fields a green table
carrying shadows.

When and where are we in this?
What push and heave swells our lives
into such change, such facing
to become as one, as two, to find places
carrying such shadows?

## 10

Leaves golden in autumn
lie in the doorway, the day's tracks.
They say something I can't hear,
strange words from a strange world.

But you see it all with your laughter,
feet in waiting dance
and the leaves and wind
make of you a girandole.

Outside it is circus time,
a fall of tumbling clowns
while I translate another ride
of years and curling anger.

## 11

See me as I am. Please
go beyond my eyes and words
and count the different faces.

You said you had many too.
So let us join the crowd,
make love before their gauntlet eyes

on the hard stones of the yard,
in the breath of hardwood coals,
in this bed and that of flaming roses.

## 12

When we arrived at the red beach
there were few sea-signs, a lip of wave,
thin noises of off-shore birds.

You'd warned me: your departure
into silence, turned face,
a private tuning.

So I took off to collect stones,
sing a little song of yearning,
while waiting for the return.

## 13

There's the long weep of casuarina,
whose branches pose in the wind
while a thread of white egrets
plies along the steepled ridge.

The run of life upon the drying plain
slows soon enough. Here we sit
in the closing Carib dark.
It speaks of death's theatre.
And you, do you read my lines?

## 14

An occasion, celebration it is,
an African tulip tree moving to colour
on a high horizon. How long will it hold
its reach against blue sky,
white houses below it?

Other questions pull me into you.
Your looking away while I talked that night
should have told me enough
to tell you to kiss me quick and go.

To be frank, open, is what you say you want
yet you look away and reply with silence.

## 15

The Brown Sugar Restaurant is best
for luncheons. Always sun in the fern forest
in which we sit, in which we hear small chatter,
the palm leaves, and watch the ferns' fine frenzy.

This is one more occasion, a comfortable exercise
in a long list of ways to forget you,
but somehow you are a face before me.
Beside me I inhale almost unwillingly,
but not quite, your fragrance of earth.

How after flying south for five hours
do I fail in what has become a comedy-crusade
of forgetting, as close as I can make it
into orbit, into other tropic faces, things?

Today I plan to travel to a new beach
where there are bath-houses and showers
and new waters unknown to love they say.

## 16

It's impossible:
finally after all those evenings
I read your silence.

As the wind strokes the chimney
while the birch fire flutters
and waves its wild arms.

Yes, it's been a translation
I was slow to make.
It's my stumbling problem.
Words fall apart
and are worthless.

Here.
Let us warm hands
against the fire's cheek.
You and I know
there will be black coals
in the morning.

## 17

Trade winds, warm from a warm sea,
where Norfolk pine and casuarina
bend inland from where I sit.

My neighbours are green lizards,
dark-eyed brown finches, doves
of mourning with the evening parade
of egrets, six o'clock following of white,
to their swamp-bed stations.

Who speaks of life and love?
Hot quivers sink in mahogany trunks.
There are day and night songs,
sung once in Ottawa, Montreal
and the Gatineau bush.
Too much. Too close. Enough
wallowing over the Carib sea.

## 18

Tree frogs in the dripping dark:
from the row of casuarina
a run of answering bells.
Yes, they sound that way
along the hidden rows
of bougainvillea, poinsettia,
allamanda.

You are somewhere, as always:
the bite of love takes hold
tasting a sharp sweetness,
but how does distance grow?
From night to morning
the taste and fragrance of you
gives strange alarums.

No, not strange, a present love
it is. The yes and no of it.

# 19

A dark toil of clouds
over a thrashing sea:
rumours of shipwrecks
out there in horizon's mouth,

just as there are cries
which, in a wrack of sleep,
play wild dream games
on a crazy stage where you
unveil in a crash of dance.

How warm and soft you are.
You lift yourself
into your own cloud music
and are followed by thousands
of winter birds. Miracle scene.

Now I hear all this
in wild singing by the armoured sea
which moves and recoils
with beating messages. Impossible love.

## 20

Chop, chop of sea
a beginning, ending,
necessary place . . .

So it was a place
in which you stood, hard
as sculpture, arms
embroidered with stars,
belt loose, slack, brighter
than Orion.

Then it was your ripe foliage,
dress of hibiscus, ginger lilies,
which brushed into flame,
a flurry of arms and fragrance.

# 21

Bird travel in casuarina trees
with light branch-music
and slur of rain birds . . .

How we then undressed
each other's eyes
and fled across a wild plain
into a flower forest
dripping with ourselves —
a surround of green flame.

There were tales in whispers,
conversations of bodies,
over and over, a drowning,
limp figures at an edge.

## 22

A certain ecstasy, backyard trumpets
bringing a march
of old and faltering parades . . .

You remember that time,
how in the white sand
certain faces appeared, magic place,
in a special past given over
to your lips wet with new honey,
warm in the afternoon.

Where are the rainbirds now?
Where is the far sun
to bring whatever our love was
to a yellow threshold?

## 23

There is a moon beyond us all,
bouquets of orchids from random suitors,
white faces at strange hours . . .

Of course it was different then.
But different from what? you ask.

Everything is that way, said someone
giving the sand-in-hand philosophers
something to grin about. Why are we
tied head and mouth by riddles?

No time for rainbows over the harbour.
There are new ships on the horizon.
Garlands of bougainvillea, allamanda
float as last rites for lovers.

## 24

Such warm questions
slip from your raving pillow-mouth
my red flamingo flower . . .

Here a slow drum-dance
fills the forest with green ghosts,
dream-stills, locked fantasies,
while your voice unfolds a story
of long voyages where lovers
undid themselves in time.

Now old songs cross the darkness.
Lights along the hill provide
a course of makeshift stars
hiding black shoals from lovers' ships.

## 25

For you I hung a "cathedral bell"
on a blue curtain above the bed
where the live memory of your body lies . . .

Love's chimes move in the wind.
This time they make a silly symphony,
a warm and crazy wordless noise
full of your madness and desire.
A heavy past we dare not carry.
Yet who'll let it go?

Thank God for a calm sea tonight,
with a light pursuit of waves
along the shore. Let's take what is
and lie together just once more.

# Love Sequence of Sorts

# Love Sequence of Sorts

## 1

The days are equal. Nothing is equal.
There is light. There is dark.
Roses rest in your lap. Your eyes speak.
Your mouth is still. There is space
between us. I think of nothing else.

## 2

Green lizard on a white wall. Caught
moment. As pendant. No. Always
the search. Lovely killer. Green baby.
The tail. The head. The quickened pulse.
The ecstasy of the fly.

# 3

"The fever of your face." René Char
said that. It is so true. Just minutes
ago the flame took over. It was
an instant of new warmth. Sudden
scale of fire. Jungle heat. Where did it go?

**4**

Talk. A screaming lot of it.
A gargle of Bristol Cream. More candles.
Finally I said my soul hurts.
You made an outpatient's enquiry.
What gives? I said my soul hurts.

## 5

On a measure of field. Over it
a harrier sweeps and toils. Behind
every hay bale is a secret. Legs
and body. Body and what breathes
with it. A waiting disaster. Count on it.

## 6

Don't even think about it. No way.
It's all touch and go from here. Only
the bite on the ear, the soft brush
leading to your inner music. Only this.
Next time we meet let's get together.

7

Fire and ice. Marriage of opposites.
Intensities. You say there's nothing wrong
in what we're doing. I listen and believe.
But the morning is a bleak wreckage.
Wrestling match in a strange nest.

## 8

Give me a break. A touch of hands
would do. Deep is the desperation.
Look at the white wall above the couch.
Red wonders from another world drip there.
They tell of wilder actions possible.

# 9

Get a life.  Sure.  Sure.  I'll get one.
Loaded. With knobs on. Stick shift
into another time-flap. Now hear this!
My brakes don't work. Where's the dimmer?
There's a leak in the tank. What's new?

## 10

Go for it. With your permission.
The crankcase is well named.
Between our legs are the seasons.
Colours replace the dark. Is that it?
Let us go now, you and I, let us go.

## 11

Think big. The giant elms and maples
torture themselves to spring. Old fires
heat the air with tired vibrations.
Now, today, a hair-trigger time, a filling
of warm tears spills into our place.

## 12

Get outa here. Okay. It's been good to know
you. To wallow. To float on a crazy sea.
To put it there. To go blank into morning.
To hear what you haven't said. Okay.
Maybe it's best. Thanks. So long.

## 13

My space. The whoop and holler
of great depths. Extremes.
Those of the inner last limits. Yes.
Inside. Go man go. Yelping team
to the warm station. Splendours.

## 14

O sparrow go on searching, pecking
my love's limp hand. Get with it.
Stay where you are. Freeze. Hop about
where her hand drops right deep. Sparrow.
No, don't shit. Go for it while I wait.

## 15

Just do it. Riddle me round.
Don't play games. Except where the world
ends. Knot me loose and tight.
There is a beginning sometime.
Forget it, baby. Call in the night.

## 16

Trust me. Wonder womb of cloud.
Breath began. Deep drench gone sour,
We limp together. What gives? Wide
spread through a glimpse of trees.
Garden of today's despair. Cool it.

# Randoms

# Lobster Pots

What happened? Well, winds began at night and blew from the east all the next day. Combers. Great white runs of white breaking one on the other. The sea kept coming all the next day. It was Tuesday. The necklaces of pots were gradually worn away and slowly heaved ashore. The marker buoys, plastic and with numbers, came in on the final waves then rolled back with the tow. Trucks came. The fishermen opened the pots some filled with crabs, lobsters and mackerel bait. There were at least six clusters of pots that morning. They quickly filled with sand. The pots were like bodies. Bodies of children. The children in ring-around-the-rosie suddenly struck. I was glad when the fishermen pulled the children ashore and piled them in trucks, then drove away. Only then did the pots cease to be children.

# Crusader

I have a membership card which allows me to swim in the pool. There are other swimmers. They too have membership cards. Certain hours are for swimmers with cards. I have never paid any attention to the rules and hours. I am not a good member. My favourite swimming time is at four in the morning. At that time I descend the stairs at the shallow end. On these occasions I wear a suit of armour. There are problems but I manage. There are no witnesses. My clanking walk on the tiles is muffled by the water. Only a faint light filters through windows at one end of the pool. My helmet is rust-proof. My whole suit is treated for underwater walking. I stay between the lines keeping a slow but steady pace. Soon there are bubbles as I approach the deep end. All is silence. At least it is for me with my helmet on. At the deep end I touch the tiles and about turn. Touch is one regulation I like. One of the ones I keep. I return until I reach the shallow waters. The bubbles vanish. At this hour I am a crusader, a tank, a walking submarine. It makes for much thought. Sometimes my helmet is very heavy. At other times it is not. I wonder if this is a problem I share with other crusaders?

# The Phoenix Game

There are no flags. The track is one-quarter of a mile and encircles the football field. It is free for anyone to use. I have never met anyone using it. I am not a jogger. My thing is fire. When I walk the track, when I am not swimming, it is aflame. It is a most enjoyable experience. The circle of flames. The buildings and houses near it light up. The heat is intense. For some reason I am not scorched. There is no pain. For someone watching from a distance it must be quite a sight. After every lap I make a mark on a large black roof which covers a rink. It is ideal for such records. Then I resume my walking. It is, of course, hotter, I think, with each lap of the track. How high the flames lap the sky. In the daylight after my walk I ask everyone I meet if they have seen the flames. No one has seen the fiery circle around the track. I listen everywhere for talk about it. No news. I wait for the weekly paper but there has been no word of it. As I say there are no flags. There is really no need of any. The fire in the darkness is colour enough. In fact it seems to remain with me as a hot fragment when I close my eyes. As one experiences after sleeping in the sun. I often look for feathers growing from my arms and legs but, really, I am only enjoying my own little phoenix game.

## Treatise on the Bumblebee

Bumblebees are always exploring and bumping into things like windows without any visible effects. They seem to be hardy and hard working. But I would venture to say they are probably quite capable of taking three-hour lunch breaks and thinking nothing of it. What else is there to say about the bumblebee?

## A Field of Wild Grasses, Daisies and Strawberries

The field is all around the cabin. The wind lives with it and is its constant companion. Towards the sea it moves with grasses, daisies and strawberries climbing a slight rise. One could say there is a constant agitation about all of this. Music comes closest to it. All of its moods. The wind changes and I read its notes in the leaning grasses. Out there waves come heaving or gently in to counter it. Or to play. The field has its nests of field sparrows and bobolinks. The birds in their song and stance broadcast a host of messages. The field-waves are alive with them. There is much to learn by watching and listening to the field of wild grasses, daisies and strawberries.

# The Upright Piano at Jolicure

The members of the orchestra have been practising all day. There is a mixed sound of strings and woodwinds. Going over stubborn or favourite passages. The players in formal dress have been ready for hours. They are diligent. They work on their own. They smile at one another. Some turn pages and go on with their practising. There is no sign of the conductor. Darkness spreads over the Jolicure marshlands and the far edges of tamarack fade. Just as the notes do of the players because they are growing tired waiting for the conductor and the invited soloist who is to play the upright piano at Jolicure.

Who will listen to the orchestra if the soloist does not appear? And, of course, there is the conductor. No audience has been invited. Perhaps next year. Wait, there is someone coming. It is a man in work clothes with the black bag of a doctor. He finds a wrench and begins intricate tuning of the upright piano. An operation. He unrolls strings, wires, and reels them off over the field, attaching them to posts of fences. The members of the orchestra watch. They smile and feel better. It is time. The man in the overalls with black bag and wrenches is after all the conductor. He raises his wrench for their attention. The orchestra begins to play. Also, the wind. The wind is soloist. It comes in from the sea and sound spills from the upright piano at Jolicure. It is the sound of the kiss of silence or, somehow, on the very edge of it.